TRAINING for the Top

Paul Mason

www.raintreepublishers.co.uk

Visit our website to find out more information about **Raintree** books.

To order:

 Phone 44 (0) 1865 888112

Send a fax to 44 (0) 1865 314091

Visit the Raintree bookshop at **www.raintreepublishers.co.uk** to browse our catalogue and order online.

First published in Great Britain by Raintree,
Halley Court, Jordan Hill, Oxford OX2 8EJ,
part of Harcourt Education.
Raintree is a registered trademark
of Harcourt Education Ltd.

© Harcourt Education Ltd 2006
First published in paperback in 2007
The moral right of the proprietor has been asserted.

Editorial: Lucy Thunder and Richard Woodham
Design: Victoria Bevan and Kamae Design
Picture Research: Melissa Allison and Lynda Lines
Production: Camilla Smith

Originated by Dot Gradations Ltd
Printed and bound in Italy by Printer Trento srl

ISBN 1 844 21457 5 (hardback)
10 09 08 07 06
10 9 8 7 6 5 4 3 2 1

ISBN 1 844 43988 7 (paperback)
11 10 09 08 07
10 9 8 7 6 5 4 3 2 1

**British Library Cataloguing in
Publication Data**
Mason, Paul
Training for the Top: Nutrition and exercise
613.7'11
A full catalogue record for this book is available from
the British Library.

Acknowledgements
The author and publishers are grateful to the
following for permission to reproduce copyright
material: Action Images/DPPI p. 5 (Franck Faugere);
Actionplus/DPPI p. 24–25 (Phillipe Millereau);
Alamy/Stock Connection p. 8–9; Corbis p. 26–27
(Tim de Waele); Empics/DPA p. 10–11; Empics/EPA p.
12–13 (Fabrice Coffrini); Empics/PA p. 6; Getty
Images/AFP pp. 14 (Javier Soriano), 15 (Jaime Reina),
22–23 (Sergei Supinsky); Getty Images p. 18–19
(Stuart Hannagan); Reuters/Scanpix p. 16–17 (Mireille
de la Lez); Rex Features/Phanie/Voisin p. 20–21;
Science Photo Library/Gusto p. 7.

Cover photograph is a portrait of swimmer Qian
Zhenhua, reproduced with permission of Empics/AP.

The publishers would like to thank Nancy Harris
and Harold Pratt for their assistance in the
preparation of this book.

Every effort has been made to contact copyright
holders of any material reproduced in this book.
Any omissions will be rectified in subsequent
printings if notice is given to the publishers.

The paper used to print this book comes from
sustainable resources.

Disclaimer
All the Internet addresses (URLs) given in this book
were valid at the time of going to press. However,
due to the dynamic nature of the Internet, some
addresses may have changed, or sites may have
changed or ceased to exist since publication. While
the author and publishers regret any inconvenience
this may cause readers, no responsibility for any
such changes can be accepted by either the author
or the publishers.

Contents

Some words are printed in bold, **like this**. You can find out what they mean on page 30. You can also look in the box at the bottom of the page where they first appear.

Peak power

The photo to the right shows cyclist Lance Armstrong. He is winning a day's racing, or **stage**, in the 2004 Tour de France. After cycling 200 kilometres (126 miles), he was still able to sprint for the finish line.

In 2003, Lance finished a stage one minute behind the winner. He had not had enough to eat and drink. His body had started to run out of **fuel**.

Like Lance, we all need food to keep our bodies healthy. But what is the difference between an ordinary person and a top athlete like Lance? Read on to find out!

TOP FACT

Cyclists call the moment when they run out of energy "bonking". Runners say they "hit the wall".

fuel something that is needed to make energy
stage one day's racing

▲ Lance Armstrong won
a record-breaking seventh
Tour de France in 2005.

Fuel in the tank

In the 1950s, many athletes ate a lot of meat. Mountain climbers would take thick pieces of steak to cook for their dinner! They thought that meat was the food that gave them most **energy**. Athletes need energy to move their bodies.

In the past, mountain climbers▼ did not always eat the foods that would give them most energy.

calorie	unit of energy
energy	ability to make a change happen
nutritionist	person who helps people to eat the right foods

Today, top athletes know more about what they should eat. **Nutritionists** help them. Nutritionists know and tell people about the right foods to eat. Nutritionists know which foods are most healthy for us.

Athletes count the **calories** in the food they eat. Calories measure the amount of energy that can be taken from food. Athletes need enough calories to train and race.

Athletes often eat ▶ foods like these to give them energy.

TOP FACT

Some top athletes use about 6,000 calories a day. An ordinary person only needs 1,500–2,000 calories!

Rowers use a lot of energy ▼
during races. Rowers need to
eat foods that have plenty of
carbohydrates, such as pasta.

carbohydrate type of food that gives us energy
fat source of energy in food, also important for looking after the body
protein part of food that helps us to grow and stay healthy

Keeping a balance

What types of food do top athletes eat? They eat a mixture of different types of food. This food log for an athlete shows what these might be:

Breakfast: porridge

Porridge has plenty of **carbohydrates**. These give the body **energy**, which it will quickly be able to use for training.

Lunch: pasta with chicken and cheese

Cheese contains **fat**. Fat is a source of energy and is also important for the body.

Dinner: rice, steamed vegetables, and grilled fish

The **proteins** in the fish (and the chicken at lunch) will help the body get back to normal after training and grow stronger.

DIFFERENT TYPES OF FOOD

Different foods have more proteins, carbohydrates, or fat:

proteins	red meat, chicken, fish, eggs, milk
carbohydrates	bread, pasta, fruit, vegetables
fat	butter, lard, margarine, oil

Eating yourself fit

Triathletes swim, cycle, and run! They have to train for three sports. Their bodies burn **energy** as they train. This energy comes from the food they have eaten. Triathletes have to "eat ahead". They do this so that they do not run out of energy during training or a race.

Triathletes eat foods containing **carbohydrates** at least an hour before training. They may eat pasta, for example. Carbohydrates give the body energy quickly. The energy from the carbohydrates will be used during training.

Triathletes also eat after training. Their bodies need more food. They need to eat before their bodies start using up their **reserves** of energy! These reserves are places where energy is stored within the body.

muscles   parts of the body that help us to move around
reserve   something that can be stored, ready to use later

▼ Triathletes need
a lot of energy.

TOP FACT

Muscles can get energy from carbohydrates faster than from other foods.

Eating yourself well

All athletes risk being injured. Athletes might crash or tear a **muscle**. They might get sick because they have been training too hard.

When injuries happen, it is very important to eat plenty of **proteins**. Proteins are found in chicken, fish, and eggs. Proteins help the body to repair itself. Getting better takes longer without enough proteins.

Athletes still need proteins even if they are not injured. Proteins help athletes' muscles to grow. Athletes' muscles get tiny tears in them during training. Proteins help repair these tears. The repaired muscles are bigger and stronger than before.

TOP FACT

Fat helps the body to avoid some injuries. Fat acts as a cushion in a crash. Fat also helps to keep the body warm.

ATHENS 2004 ⃝⃝⃝⃝⃝

▼Gail Devers is a top athlete.
She was injured in the 2004
Olympic Games.

Food into fitness

Why are all these top athletes out training so hard? It is because they want to get fitter! But what does "getting fitter" really mean?

Your body needs **energy** to be able to move. This energy comes from **nutrients** in food. Nutrients move around the body in the blood. Blood is pumped around the body by the heart. So an athlete needs to make their heart stronger to pump plenty of blood around.

Oxygen is a gas found in air. We need oxygen to help us get energy from food. Our bodies get oxygen when we breathe air into our **lungs**. Athletes need to make their lungs stronger. They can then breathe in more oxygen.

Athletes train to make their **muscles** stronger. Building up muscles uses even more nutrients, especially **carbohydrates** and **proteins**.

lungs	parts of the body that we use when we breathe
nutrients	parts of food that we need for growth and energy
oxygen	gas found in air

On and on

Most people think a **marathon** is a long way to run. But for some long-distance runners, a marathon is almost a sprint!

Ultra runners compete in races that can last all day and night. Some races are over 160 kilometres (100 miles) long. Ultra runners have to keep getting **oxygen** and **nutrients** to their **muscles**. Otherwise, they will run out of **energy**. Ultra runners train so they have:

✗ a strong heart. The heart is a muscle. Just like leg or arm muscles, you can build up a stronger heart. A strong heart moves blood to your muscles better.

✗ bigger **lung capacity**. This means their **lungs** can take in more air with each breath. Their bodies can get more oxygen.

lung capacity	maximum amount of air you can fit into your lungs
marathon	race of 42.2 kilometres (26.6 miles)

▼ *This race is held in the Arctic Circle. It is very cold. The signpost warns runners to watch out for the polar bears in the area!*

Gjelder hele Svalbard

17

Making a splash

Swimmers like this Olympic racer train by swimming up to 50 kilometres (31 miles) a week. They are **endurance** athletes. Endurance athletes race over long distances.

Swimmers and other endurance athletes train their heart, **lungs**, and **muscles**. They do this by swimming, running, or cycling for a long time. They might train for 4 hours each day.

18

endurance   ability to do the same thing for a long time

Endurance athletes do not train at full speed. They train at a speed that they can keep up for a long time. This gets their muscles, heart, and lungs used to having to work hard for a long time.

▼ This swimmer is training for a race. She is wearing special paddles on her hands. Among other things, the paddles help her muscles get stronger.

TOP FACT

Your body recovers faster if you do some gentle exercise after training instead of just resting!

The heart of training

This athlete is wearing an HRM, or Heart Rate Monitor. It is a machine that measures how fast someone's heart is beating. HRMs record the number of times the heart beats each minute.

The heart is very important for fitness. It is the **muscle** that pumps blood around the body. The blood takes **nutrients** and **oxygen** to other muscles. This gives them **energy** to do more work.

Top athletes use HRMs to tell how fast their heart is beating. A fast heart beat tells them they are training really hard. If they are recovering after a race, they might not want to work so hard. This means keeping their heart rate slower. The HRM will tell them if their heart starts to beat too quickly.

The small screen ▶ shows how many times the heart beats each minute.

Building strength

Athletes like this weightlifter need to train for power, not long-distance effort. Weightlifters compete in different classes depending on how heavy they are. The best weightlifters have a lot of **muscle** power. But they are not very heavy.

Weightlifters build up their muscles by lifting heavy weights. They lift the weights just a few times each day in training. Weightlifters often train by lifting close to the heaviest weight they can. This gets them ready for competitions.

Weightlifters build up powerful muscles that are large and thick. Their muscles can lift huge weights. They can lift huge weights only a few times in a row. They do not have as much **endurance** as a **marathon** runner. A weightlifter's muscles are very different from the slim muscles of a marathon runner.

Top Fact

Halil Mutlu, from Turkey, weighed under 56 kilograms (9 stone), but he once lifted 168 kilograms (26 stone). That's more than three times his body weight!

▼ *Weightlifters need to eat plenty of **protein**. This helps their muscles grow bigger.*

23

Sprinters train using ▼
quick bursts of energy.

Speed freaks

Sprinters run fast over short distances. Like weightlifters, sprinters need powerful **muscles**. Sprinters use weight training to build their muscles. Unlike weightlifters, sprinters need to be able to move quickly. Most weightlifters would not make very good sprinters!

Sprinters build up their speed and power by running on the track. They train as hard and fast as possible. When training, they do not race many times in a row.

SPRINTER TRAINING DIARY
- warm up – stretching, gentle running
- 10 lots of sprints at 90 per cent of full speed
- gentle running
- warm down

Sprinters are not **endurance** athletes. Sprinters do not train to run long distances. A sprint race is over so fast that the muscles don't have time to run out of **energy**.

The finishing line

Remember the first page, where Lance Armstrong sprinted to victory? Being able to sprint wasn't all he needed. Lance also had to ride over 200 kilometres (126 miles) up and down the mountains. He needed **endurance**, as well as power.

Most top athletes are like Lance. They need power and endurance. A few athletes are real specialists, though:

- Weightlifters need big **muscles** with lots of power. They don't need as much endurance.

- Ultra runners need strong hearts and **lungs**. Ultra runners need more endurance than power.

- Swimmers and football players are somewhere in between.

Whichever group they fall into, all top athletes plan their diet and exercise very carefully!

26

Healthy eating

This chart gives you an idea of how much of each type of food you need to eat each day. As well as eating healthily, you should do sport often.

Food groups	Examples	
Grains	Whole wheat bread, English muffin, pitta bread, bagels, cereals, oatmeal, crackers	
Vegetables	Tomatoes, potatoes, carrots, green peas, broccoli, turnips, spinach	
Fruit	Apricots, bananas, dates, grapes, oranges, orange juice, peaches	
Low-fat or fat-free dairy foods	Fat-free or low-fat milk, low-fat and fat-free cheese	
Meat, poultry, fish	Fat-free and skin-free meat is healthiest.	
Nuts, seeds, legumes	Almonds, peanuts, walnuts, sunflower seeds, lentils	
Fat and oils	Soft margarine, low-fat mayonnaise, light salad dressing	
Sweets	Jelly, jam, ice cream	

Serving sizes	A fairly active 9–13 year old	Why?
1 slice bread, 28 g (1 oz) dry cereal, 0.5 cup cooked rice/pasta/cereal	6–8 servings per day	Grains give you **energy**.
1 cup raw leafy vegetables, 0.5 cup cooked vegetables	3–5 servings per day	Vegetables contain lots of **nutrients**.
170 g (6 oz) fruit juice, 1 medium piece of fruit, 0.25 cup dried fruit, 0.5 cup fresh/frozen/canned fruit	4–5 servings per day	Fruit contains lots of nutrients.
227 g (8 oz) milk, 1 cup yoghurt, 43 g (1.5 oz) cheese	2–3 servings per day	Eating dairy foods gives your body protein.
85 g (3 oz) cooked meats, poultry, or fish	1–2 servings per day	Meat, poultry, and fish give your body **protein**.
43 g (1.5 oz) nuts, 14 g (0.5 oz) seeds, 0.5 cup cooked dry beans or peas	3–5 servings per day	Nuts, seeds, and legumes contain protein and give your body energy.
1 tsp soft margarine, 1 tsp vegetable oil	2–3 servings per week	Too much of this group is bad for you.
1 tablespoon sugar, 227 g (8 oz) lemonade	0–2 servings per week	Sweets should be low in fat. Too many are bad for you.

Glossary

calorie unit of energy. Eating the right number of calories is important for a healthy diet.

carbohydrate type of food that gives us energy. Pasta contains carbohydrates.

endurance ability to do the same thing for a long time. Long-distance runners need endurance.

energy ability to make a change happen. Athletes need energy to move their muscles.

fat source of energy in food, also important for looking after the body. Too much fat is bad for the body and can be unhealthy.

fuel something that is needed to make energy

lung capacity maximum amount of air you can fit into your lungs. Athletes train to make their lung capacity bigger.

lungs parts of the body that we use when we breathe. Oxygen goes from our lungs into our blood.

marathon race of 42.2 kilometres (26 miles). Marathon runners are endurance athletes.

muscles parts of the body that help us to move around. Muscles get bigger and smaller to pull and push the parts of the body that they are joined to.

nutrients parts of food that we need for growth and energy. Different nutrients do different jobs in the body including helping growth or repairing damage.

nutritionist person who helps people to eat healthy foods

oxygen gas found in air. Oxygen helps our bodies get energy from food.

protein part of food that helps us to grow and stay healthy. Dairy foods contain protein.

reserve something that can be stored, ready to use later. A person's body has reserves of energy.

stage one day's racing. The Tour de France is made up of many stages.

Want to know more?

Books

- *Eyewitness: Food*, Laura Buller (Dorling Kindersley, 2005)
- *The Making of a Champion* series (Heinemann Library, 2004)

Fitness testing

- Your local sports centre may be able to help you find out how well your heart and lungs are working.

Websites

- www.uci.ch is the website of cycling's international governing body. It has advice on training and information about top riders. It can also help you get in touch with your own national cycling organization.

- www.lancearmstrong.com tells you about the most successful Tour de France rider ever. There is also a section on the Lance Armstrong Foundation, which works to help people who have cancer.

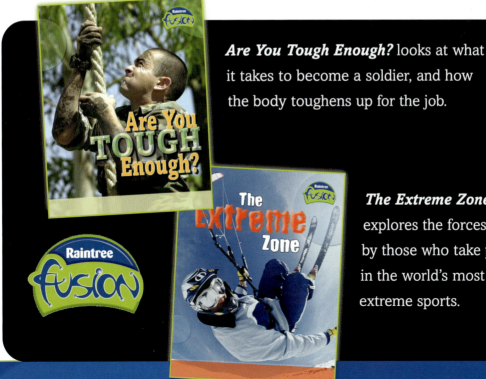

Are You Tough Enough? looks at what it takes to become a soldier, and how the body toughens up for the job.

The Extreme Zone explores the forces used by those who take part in the world's most extreme sports.

Index